Sacred Arts:
Astronomy Geometry Numerology Sacred Sacred **Sacred!!!**

by
(Ozryuwyzir)
Apostle OlegMB

Invitation:

"giving and receiving"

Cup of Cold water

to a prophet.

469 450 6743

evangelistoleg@

gmail.com

About nature of my Art
Uniqueness of my books
they are one of kind you cant find
them no where else!!!!!!!

Just as there is abstract art
do you get it? half of the the time
your eyes is crossed, trying to
understand it?
Just like there is hip-hop

do you understand it?
You pay money for it
do they use perfect English? Aint
nothing perfect in them relics
matter fact they curse in it!!
Just like they got they form of art
I got mine.
" I GOT REAL KEYS,KEYS!!!"

About the Author:
Apostle Oleg MB
Feminist Theologian
Author Incubator
Loving Person
Well Traveled
Divinely Spoiled
Sacred Scientist

Prophetic Soul Physician
Soul Doctor
Living Conductor.
One of a kind Author
Founder of School of Mystery

Introduction

In 1997 it all started it was given to me to pursue this precious direction. Long process became to be exciting as I would never have imagined. From 1990 to 1997 I was so hesitant to pursue this

all was changed (with Blood of Jesus, His Guidance) with Just one definition: According to Wikipedia:
Sacred geometry involves **sacred** universal patterns used in the design of everything in our reality, most often seen in **sacred** architecture and **sacred** art. The basic belief is that **geometry** and mathematical ratios, harmonics and proportion are also found in music, light, cosmology.

As I was traveling being new at this; I knew Jesus and him crucified I believed in the cross (still do). Cross was my focus, yet I started to notice more and more different signs on buildings and particularly on church buildings. It was alarming and confusing yet the Lord said to me: "pursue this I will be glorified in this". My research started to take momentum since 1997, particularly: Sacred astronomy, sacred numerology, sacred architecture, as well as sacred literature have one thing in common not any ordinary person or lay person can be allowed to approach these HOLY SCIENCES.. THIS IS VERY VERY IMPORTANT.

Chapter 1 Sacred arts of a man and woman..

"be enthusiastic on the door #99 as you were on the door #1)"

Unknown

What is it means to be human? What qualifies you to be human?

"Philosophy," writes Sir William Hamilton, "has been defined [as]: The science of things divine and human, and of the causes in which they are contained [Cicero]; The science of effects by their causes [Hobbes]; The science of sufficient reasons [Leibnitz]; The science of things possible, inasmuch as they are possible [Wolf]; The science of things evidently deduced from first principles [Descartes]; The science of truths, sensible and abstract [de Condillac]; The application of reason to its legitimate objects [Tennemann]; The science of the relations of all knowledge to the necessary ends of human reason [Kant];The science of the original form of the ego or mental self [Krug]; The science of sciences [Fichte]; The science of the absolute [von Schelling]; The science of the absolute indifference of the ideal and real [von Schelling]--or, The identity of identity and nonidentity

[Hegel]." (See Lectures on Metaphysics and Logic.)
This is what they wise of this world say about life in some sum. I am not going that way I am interested in what thus saith the Lord High and Mighty who sits on the throne and loughs at the elite of the land. Scripture first.
1Cor15:46- spiritual came later 1st it was physical.
These are just few paradigms that people follow: here are just a few:
Human: food, work, fun, friends, life, kids, etc;

Human: career, coworkers, drinks, food
Human: family, food, fun, religion
Human: God, ministry, raid/travel, research, rest, write, and repeat;
Human: relationship, house, work for bills, get away 2 weeks in the year.
Human: arts, creating, meeting people, reading books,
there is a way that seemeth right to the man or woman but what about the end ???????
in the sacred arts of Humanity is :

<u>self definition</u>
<u>law of self space</u>
<u>self manifestation</u>
<u>self creation</u>
<u>self incarnation</u>
<u>science of self knowledge</u>

just as one of the incentives is unprecedented flow of money to you. Making money off of who you are as opposed to what you do. This great separation is created by Servile Arts induced by different schools of corporate giants and thus forcing (for example) to quit farming in east Texas . This particular farmer had cows and milk farm/plant but now it is abandoned and left as monument of the past. Self-assurance of self realization, self incarnation and self manifestation is everything. **When laws of universe are not appropriated and one is not aligned to the stars as well as one is not conscious of his subconsciousness and consciousness** then the whole world starts erupting tsunamis of waves of self doubt inhibiting one to abandon everything pertaining to his or her self manifestation; incarnating that which one had in the eternity past- even though That person is saved and going to heaven- Jesus done paid for it. (do not loose appetite of a hungry immigrant who just came to USA). **Jesus had to incarnate who he was before the foundation of the world. So do you. Jesus did so you know for sure you can do it.** " as Jesus was so are we in this world" - 1 John. The "works that I do even the greater ones shall you do"- Gospel of John.

The whole book can be summoned in one phrase of just a one question in

Genesis:..."Who *told* thee that thou wast naked?"

The prosperity of soul is at stake I am writing this book and being inspired by God thinking how to enrich you all souls. This is what I am talking about here dear ladies and gentlemen.

"There is
a natural body and there is a spiritual body" (1 Corinthians 15:44)

Chapter 2

John 10:34King James Version (KJV)

34 Jesus answered them, Is it not written in your law, I said, Ye are gods?

35 If he called them gods, unto whom the word of God came, and the scripture cannot be broken;

"Stop chasing what they call HOT PASSION OF THE MOMENT!!"

KNOW YOUR MYSTERY AND YOU MY FRIEND ARE CHOSEN IN IT!!!!!!!!

Socrates (469-399 BC) Of God he said: "What He is I know not; what He is not I know.

This man as sincere as he was at the peak of his age was short of this great mystery, God is a mystery in many ways.

Mystery

"The Mystery of Christ" (3:4);
"The Mystery of His Will" (1:9);
"The Great Mystery" (5:32 as it is in Greek); and
"The Mystery of God, Christ" (Colossians 2:2).

KNOW THAT GOD HAS DONE EVERYTHING FOR YOU TO BE BEST YOU

<u>through the process of self incarnation of creator manifestation from inside out.</u>

Here what you should know about God for you, in you and through you.

Leviticus 3:16

And the priest shall burn them on the altar as food offered by fire for a pleasing odor. All fat is the LORD's.

Let us first look at four of the common Old Testament names for the Deity: *El, Eloah, Elyon,* and *Elohim* (and we will consider another "*El Shadday*" at the end of the Report).

El Shadday

As for "*El Shadday,*" it means "the Almighty who is All-Sufficient." In combination with *El* (singular) and *Shadday* (plural) it occurs 7 times (*e.g.* Genesis 17:1), and alone it is "the All-Sufficient," 41 times in the Old Testament.

Adon

There is also *Adon* (singular) which means Sovereign, Lord, Master, Possessor. It occurs 30 times (*e.g.* Exodus 23:17).

Adonahy

Then there is *Adonahy* (plural, perhaps like *Elohim*) which means the same as *Adon* and it occurs about 200 times (*e.g.* Genesis 15:2, 8).

Yahweh

Since we are informed in the Book of Revelation that the word YHWH actually means "**was, is** [or being], **coming**" (Revelation 1:4), the English meaning of "Yahweh" is something like the "Continually Existing One,"

El

El as a title occurs about 250 times. It is singular and it means "strong" and "mighty." An English phrase that could adequately denote the Hebrew meaning: "the Mighty One."

Eloah

Eloah (singular) is from the word *ahlah,* to worship, **to adore and the word represents the power who is to be worshiped.** It occurs 56 times. An English phrase that denotes it is "the Adorable One."

Elyon

Elyon (singular) denotes the power who possesses. It occurs 36 times. In English it could be rendered "the Most High Owner."

*****Elohim*****

In Ecclesiastes 12:1 the actual reading of the Hebrew is: "**Remember your *Creators*** [plural] **in the days of your youth.**"

- In Job 35:10: “**None say, ‘Where is God my *Makers*’** [plural]?”

- Notice also Proverbs 9:10: “**The knowledge of the Holy Ones** [plural] **is understanding.**”

- In Isaiah 54:5 the words “**Maker**” and “**Husband**” are both plural in Hebrew.

- Also note the use of “**Holy Ones**” (rendered *saints* in the King James) in Job 5:1 — and the same plural construction occurs in Hosea 11:12.

- In Isaiah 6:8 there is a plural noun and pronoun describing God. “**Also I** [Isaiah] **heard the voice of the Lord** [<u>*Lords*</u> — *adonay,* plural, the same <u>*Lords,*</u> plural, as Isaiah

6:1], **saying, Whom shall I** [singular] **send, and who will go for us** [plural]?"

- Godhead said when they got angry with the people building the tower at Babel. God said: "**Let *us* go down and confound their language**" (Genesis 11:7).

Jesus Christ died but not to abolish the laws of nature such as Law of gravity etc.

***Elohim* (plural) of *Eloah* and occurs some 2700 times.** This word in English really means "**the Mighty Ones.**" This is a most difficult word to render in English because it most often in the Old Testament takes singular verbs and adjectives (not always, however, because **in Genesis 1:26 it is connected with plural verb. and pronouns**).

It is the word "Dynasty."

As far as Supreme Deity is concerned, ***Elohim* means a Divine Family (a Dynasty). (Ephesians 3:14–15)**. **"In the beginning, *the Dynasty* created the heaven and the earth"** (Genesis 1:1). Or, for verse 26: **"Then *the Dynasty* said, Let *us* make man in our image, after our likeness."** In both cases, the word "Dynasty" contains both the singular and plural aspects that *Elohim* possesses,

> **"And *the Dynasty* spoke all these words saying, I am Yahweh *your Dynasty*** [the one who heads "your Dynasty"], **who brought you out of the land of Egypt. You shall have no other *Dynasty* before me,** [etc.]."
>
> - *Exodus 20:1–3*

And in Shema, it would be: **"Hear, Oh Israel, Yahweh *our Dynasty* is one**

Yahweh" (Deuteronomy 6:4). And Isaiah 45:5 would be: "**I am Yahweh, and there is no other, besides me there is no Dynasty** [that truly rules]." "**I say, you are a *Dynasty,* children of the Most High, all of you**" (Psalm 82:5

YOU ARE NOT JUST YOU SIGULAR YOU – YOU ARE ONE OF THE IMPORTANT PARTS OF DYNASTY. KNOW THAT.
GOD AND YOU ARE COLABORERS!!!

Jeremiah 3:16And when you have multiplied and increased in the land, in those days, says the LORD, they shall no more say, "The ark of the covenant of the LORD." It shall not come to mind, or be remembered, or missed; it shall not be made again.

This is the wisdom of saints.

The number one craving of the your, your soul I am talking to you about your soul, the number one craving of your own soul is to experience God. The number two craving of the soul is to fit your body perfectly and use body to the fullest of its capacity enjoying all God creation and as part of enjoying Gods creation redeem them if they need to be redeem by the blood of the Lamb.

Contrary to many Stoic Christian believe that states: *good and evil being contrary, both are necessary since each sustains the other. I do not believe that for a moment.* **God is alone is good do not need evil to sustain good. I am not in perpetual war as many affirm. 911!!!!!!! KEY: After Jesus' death on the cross no none has to loose for me to win and for Gospel to go forth in full speed accomplishing all**

<u>God send it to do, with no sweat and no resistance for who straighten out that which God made it crooked. Amen.</u>

Chapter 3
NUMEROLOGY

"the utterance of a thought."

"He has made my mouth as a sharp sword..." (Isaiah 49:2). Ephesians 6:17:

John 21:11

Numerology is the universal language. People who might be speaking two different languages because they were born in two different countries. Numbers don't lie - they always tell what is sum in value, meaning, significance, common dominator and amount

For example Bible tells us exact number of fish- read:

"Simon Peter went up and drew the net to land, full of large fish, a hundred and fifty-three; and although th:ere were so many, the net was not torn."

153 is not just accident number in the holy Bible it is powerful number in all dimensions, and in all worlds.

square root of 153 is 12.369 is the number of full moons per year. That is why Bible astronomy, numerology and God have everything to do with everything to the slightest detail.

IT IS ALL NUMBERS

AND NUMBERS DONT LIE!!!!!!!!!!!

The Latin adage, "Omnia in numeris sita sunt" means: "Everything lies veiled in numbers."

Brothers and sisters, Ladies and gentlemen I am not writing things of opposite ends., oh no!

I am past that!!!!!!! this stuff is for babies.

I past that !!!!!!!!!!!!!!!!!!!!!!!!!!!!

According to dictionary:

Eclecticism may be defined as the practice of choosing apparently irreconcilable doctrines from antagonistic

schools. This is for babies. I am past that. This is where denominations reside. Numerology as well as other sciences in my books and in my research do not belong to this or other categories like that. "let God be true and every man a liar!!!!"

the key question is what I think about what God things about this subject. And Bible are the thoughts of God.

Luke 21:15King James Version (KJV)

15 For I will give you a mouth and wisdom, which all your adversaries shall not be able to gainsay nor resist.

How does this dynasty is established there are levels.
1st all creation is waiting for the manifestations of the sons of God or dynasty:
CELEBRATION OF SACRED CALENDAR SHOULD BE INCLUDED WITH THIS STUDY OF SACRED NUMEROLOGY.
one day is as 1,000 years to the Lord." (2 Pet 3:8)
what does that supposed to me.
Plz do not miss this!!!!!!!!!

You are creating your reality of heaven's realms here and now. **One day here on earth and what you do here and now creates 1000 years in other realms for what you bind here on earth will be bound in heaven.** So what a thousand years you are creating this day , this day , imagine what you one minute will cost you or what % it will pay you. Your minutes matter!!!this is what principle of sowing and reaping is all about !!!!

LETS CONTINUE TO PLAY NUMBERS GAME

There are 7 in the head, 2 nostrils, 2 eyes, 2 ears, and a mouth;

so in the heavens there are 2 favorable stars, 2 unpropitious, 2 luminaries, and Mercury alone undecided. In nature, such as the 7 metals, division of the week into 7 days, and

have named them from the 7 planets.

12-12 gates, 12 months, 12 apostles, 12 stones.
22-Bible and 22 . . From the first epistle, Romans, to the end is 22 books. This is Canon Wheel. The Bible may be divided into three sections of 22 books each . There are 22 letters in the Hebrew alphabet. Revelation ends the whole Bible on a 22nd chapter

4-There are 4 horsemen of the Apocalypse. There are 4 angels standing ready at the 4 corners of Earth.
There are 4 Gospels, 4 living beasts in Ezekiel, Daniel, and Revelation

21- 21 chapters in the Gospel of John. There are three epistles of John, with 5, 1, and 1 chapters respectively. 5 plus 1 plus 1 equals 7, times 3 epistles equals 21. In the Revelation of John, there are 3 dispensations of God's wrath, first 7 seals, then 7 trumpets, then 7 bowls of wrath. 7 times 3 equals 21.

A FEW INTERPRETATIONS OF SYMBOLIC NUMBERS

(Based on *Number in Scripture* by E. W. Bullinger)

ONE...Unity and Primacy.

TWO.......................................Difference and Division.

THREE.....................Divine Perfection and Completeness.

FOUR..............................Earthy Creation and Division.

FIVE...Grace.

SIX..Man.

SEVEN..Full or Satisfied.

EIGHT..................Regeneration, a New Beginning, Jesus.

NINE...Finality or Judgement.

TEN.............................the Perfection of Divine Order.

ELEVEN...............Disorder, Imperfection, Disintegration.

TWELVE...........Organization and Government Perfection.

FORTY..........................Probation, Trial, Chastisement.

SEVENTY.................................Perfect Spiritual Order.

ONE HUNDRED AND FIFTY-THREE.........Christ's Elect.

SIX HUNDRED AND SIXTY-SIX..............the Antichrist.

EIGHT HUNDRED AND EIGHTY-EIGHT................Jesus.

based on Bullinger I see that there are some truths nevertheless it is just primary numerology. There are depth and length if one was to dig deeper.

Apostle Paul as well as other apostles had to deal with Epicureans Stoics and Pythagorianism. This was the most desired society of brilliant minds and or brains of that age. They had a lot to say about many things yet Paul was brilliant in his own way He knew the True Way. He knew that Most of these usages of numbers and astro-numerological things are basically commercial indulgences and notorious: break and gas pedal with each so called holiday. To the degree that human individuality is so torn apart from within. Personal few applications of what I call sacred numerology. This is not exhaustive but just a beginning of what I can introduce of this great mystery at this time.

Most of churches and or **Christian world are Baconians. Yes you heard me right!!!!!!!! They are Baconians that is inductive, system of reasoning (whereby facts are arrived at by a process of observation and verified by experimentation**

Seriously this is not new system. It helps you in this age. But really you gonna bring this to Christ likeness???? Heavens no!!!!!!!!!!!!!!

2) 6000- ruer of ever the legion
3) 10,000- you David ad 10,000 of us, Or what king, going to make war against another king, sitteth not down first, and consulteth whether he be able with ten thousand to meet him that cometh against him with twenty thousand? Luke 14:31

4) one of the high priest (true one) said to Russian army you lost the war in Afghanistan because you fought it on physical level and they were fighting on other 2 dimensions. They fought you from Gobi desert around Afghanistan, with the intelligent that would enlist and exercise the the venues of special favors with other high demi-gods to make economical deals that would have mutual consequential benefits of gigantic proportions. That was done by invoking entities of unknown origins to you as person or to you general.

According to Carl Munck we get next table of numerology

Carl listed some of the Gematrian numbers with their "Alpha" or "Word" meanings in the newsletter -

144 = Light

288 = Double light, the Kingdom of Heaven.

432 = Consecration (also the square root of the classical speed of light, 186624 miles per second). Several Biblical references are also tied to it; Luke 8:15, Revelation 2:17, etc.

396 = Classical earth radius (3960 miles).

576 = Prophecy and Gospel.

864 = Time (2) the source of light and life, (3) Most Holy.

1152 = Witness (576 x 2). Biblical references include Luke 14:26, Revelation 3:12, 12:11 and 19:9.

1296 = Circle of space (360 x 60 x 60). 1296 was also Plato's favorite number.

1548 = Priest of God.

1728 = A-flat in music.

2304 = False Christs and False prophets (1 Cor. 14:22, Mark 13:12).

3168 = Lord Jesus Christ.

3888 = New Jerusalem (Rev. 21:2, 1 Cor. 12:27, Luke 8:21, etc.).

5184 = Victory over the beast (Rev. 15:2).

This might be too much for some of you; yet some of you **of Vicoism, ohh yes Lutherans, Methodist and other all who abolish all spiritual and miraculous workings of God.. These**

sects are all living according toGiovanni Battista Vico, who held that God controls His world not miraculously but through natural law. The laws by which men rule themselves. This is History my friend that past Ideologies are alive and well in creeds and walls of the Churches (more about the walls of Cathedrals later in the book)

Let me get back to more basic of Sacred Numerology: 9 fruits of the Spirit: (Gal 5.22,23). The are NINE gifts of the Spirit (1 Cor 12.8-10) and NINE Beatitudes (Mat 5.3-11). Jesus completed His work on the cross "about the NINTH hour" (Mat 27.46). The sum of the numeric values of the 22 letters of the Hebrew alphabet is 4995 = 5 × 999.

all I SAY TO YOU IS WATCH, WATCH AND PRAY

SEARCH THE SCRIPTURES ,,,,..!!!!

No.	Meaning
1	Unity; New beginnings
2	Union; Division; Witnessing
3	Divine completeness and perfection
4	Creation; The world; Creative works
5	Grace; God's goodness; Pentateuch (first five books)
6	Weakness of man; Manifestation of sin ; Evils of Satan
7	Resurrection; Spiritual completeness; Fathers perfection
8	New birth; New beginnings
9	Fruit of the spirit; Divine completeness from the Father
10	Testimony; Law and responsibility
11	Disorder and judgment
12	Governmental perfection
13	Apostasy; depravity and rebellion

4	**Deliverance; Salvation**
5	**Rest**
6	**Love**
7	**Victory**
8	**Bondage**
9	**Faith**
0	**Redemption**
1	**Exceeding sinfulness of sin**
2	**Light**
3	**Death**
4	**The Priesthood**
5	**Repentance; The forgiveness of sins**
6	**The Gospel of Christ**
7	**Preaching of the Gospel**
8	**Eternal life**
9	**Departure**
0	**Blood of Christ; Dedication**
1	**Offspring**
2	**Covenant**
3	**Promise**
4	**Naming of a son**
5	**Hope**

36	Enemy
37	The word of our Father
38	Slavery
39	Disease
40	Trials; Probation; Testings
42	Israel's oppression; First advent
44	Judgment of the World
45	Preservation
50	Holy Spirit; Pentecost
60	Pride
66	Idol worship
70	Punishment and restoration of Israel; Universality
100	Election; Children of the promise
119	Spiritual perfection and victory 7*17=119
120	Divine period of probation
144	The Spirit guided life
200	Insufficiency
600	Warfare
666	Antichrist
777	Christ
888	Holy Spirit; The sum of Tree of Life
1000	Divine completeness and Fathers glory

00	Salvation of the world through the blood of the Lamb (Those who chose between Christ and Antichrist)
00	Deception of Antichrist; Second advent
00	Final judgment; Zadok
000	Those numbered of Israel

Do the numbers rule the World, yes!!! and people who proficient in numbers rule the world through the numbers.

Chapter 4

SACRED ASTRONOMY!!!!

Jeremiah 2:16Moreover, the men of Memphis and Tah'panhes have broken the crown of your head.

Do not let them do that again!!!!!!!!!!!!!

Sacred Astronomy for all intended purposes of what I am talking about here I am approaching from strictly of Biblical sense otherwise known what God thinks about it and I know his thoughts because of what He wrote in Holy Word.

God's creation ultimately speaks of God and his Glory as well as of his plans. Thus the wisemen decoded the location of the Birth of Son of God based upon the stars, or astronomy. What was said of Messiah in Holy Word was also known that in the stars that is why wise men were able to find the Location of Messiah.

They mystery is great it took me to come through the cracks of time of centuries of hidden exposition and mysteries untold with the human brain. **There are four Gospels of one Jesus . There are many Zodiac signs of one God at least three I will show you from the Bible**.

1) First set of signs of Zodiac The 12 signs of Jesus in the starts can be read the the heavens book: it is all there!!!!

1. **Virgo** - the virgin will give birth to son. Virgin Birth of Jesus Christ.
2. **Libra** - the scales - the judgment of Jesus Christ on the Cross by God the Father to pay for the sins of the world and satisfy the Justice of God.
3. **Scorpius** - the scorpion - satan, the enemy of Jesus Christ who inspired the crucifixion,

4. **Sagittarius** - the archer - the Redeemer's victory over Satan at the Cross.
5. **Capricornus** - the goat - the sin offering which provided unlimited atonement for the sins
6. **Aquarius** - the water man - showers of blessing from Heaven.
7. **Pisces** - the two fish - one pointing toward the pole star and the other toward the Ecliptic symbolize a priest interceding for the believer and foreshadow Jesus Christ, the High Priest of the Church.

8. **Aries -** the ram - Christ as the Conqueror Commander-in-Chief with the resurrected Church in Heaven during the Tribulation.
9. **Taurus -** the bull - The Redeemer will return at the Second Advent

10. **Gemini** - the twins - the story of Esau's attack of Jacob expanded into the Tribulation when Israel's enemies seek to destroy it.

11. **Cancer** - the crab - eternal security, "in Adam all die, even so by agency of Christ shall all be made alive" (1 Cor 15:22)

12. **Leo -** the lion - The Lord Jesus Christ as the Lion of the Tribe of Judah who returns to rule in the Millennium and cast the devil into the Lake of Fire.

Weapon of Stars is given to us by Almighty God to use and take full advantage of the full Armor of Creator and not just the full Armor of God. Full Armor of Creator includes: sacred

astronomy, sacred numerology and etc.

Amos 5:8 King James Version

Seek him that maketh the seven stars and Orion, and turneth the shadow of death into the morning, and maketh the day dark with night: that calleth for the waters of the sea, and poureth them out upon the face of the earth: The LORD is his name:

AS YOU SEE WE ARE COMMANDED TO SEEK GOD THE MAKER OF CERTAIN HEAVENLY BODIES

Job 9:9King James Version (KJV)

9 Which maketh Arcturus, Orion,
and Pleiades, and the chambers of
the south.

You do not need to be a scholar to go through 12 months and tell the story of Gods redemption based upon the 12 signs of Zodiacs; the issue is that many other dimensions of the signs of circle of Gods story as we see in the stars.

2) Second Zodiac sign of Biblical proportions: The 12 sons are also 12 signs and function as 12 'doors'

Genesis 49 Jacob states about his children that corresponds to the signs of the zodiac with the names of the 12 tribes:

being the first sign of the zodiac, 'presses upon their heel' in the circular zodiac.]

<u>Asher,</u> 'the weigher of bread,' is Libra (the Scales)

<u>Nephtali,</u> 'a hind let loose,' is Capricorn (the Goat)

<u>Joseph,</u> 'whose bow abides in strength,' is Sagittarius (the Archer)

<u>Benjamin,</u> 'ravening as a wolf, devouring his prey by morning, dividing the spoil at night,' is Cancer (the Crab)

The 12 sons have been named but one sign remains-<u> Virgo (the Virgin). This sign is 'veiled,' and is correlated with Dinah,</u> Jacob's

daughter (Gen 30:21). the name of the first sign was 'Gad/Aries'; the second sign was 'Issachar/Taurus', etc.

An other point is clearly seen in the book of Revelation, you will see that it is not to be taken lightly yet churches and and astronomy is intimate in nature in all aspects of life in a person, peoples, tongues, tribes and nations.

Revelation1:11 Saying, I am the Alpha and Omega, the first and last and what thou seest, write in a book, and send it unto the seven churches which are inAsia, Ephesus, and unto Smyrna, and unto Pergamos and unto Thyatira, and

unto Philadelphia, and unto Laodicea. Revelation 1:20 The mystery of the seven stars which thous sawest in my right hand, and the seven golden candlesticks. The seven stars are the angels of the seven churches and the seven candlesticks which thou sawest are the seven churches.

Job 38:31King James Version (KJV)

31 Canst thou bind the sweet influences of Pleiades, or loose the bands of Orion?

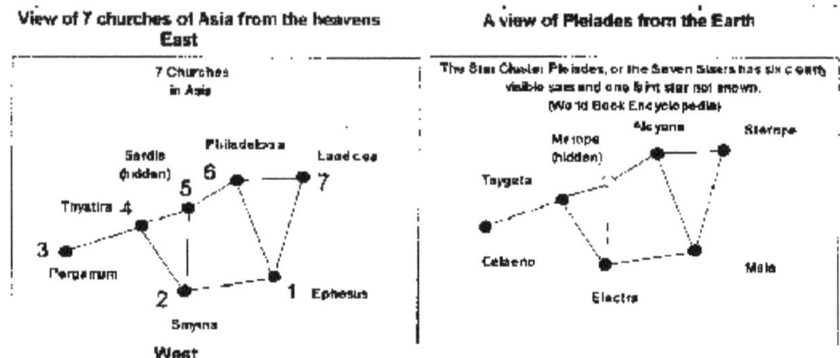

So you see that seven churches are the 7 stars Pleiades, they are angels of Daniel 12. this is powerful.

Job 38:32King James Version (KJV)

32 Canst thou bring forth Mazzaroth in his season? or canst thou guide Arcturus with his sons?**Job 26:13King James Version (KJV)**

13 By his spirit he hath garnished the heavens; his hand hath formed the crooked serpent. (Constellation

I believe that Bible itself in Job give us the other 12 SIGNS OF ZODIAC OR CIRLCE; PLEASE CONSIDER NEXT:

However in Job 38:31-32 we read, "Canst thou bind the sweet influences of Pleiades, or loose the bands of Orion? Canst thou bring forth Mazzaroth in his season? or canst thou guide Arcturus with his sons?" Mazzaroth is a Hebrew word which means "the constellations of the Zodiac."

3) there is a third circle or Zodiac of Biblical proportions;

Hidden in plain sight in Job chapters 38 and 39, are given the twelve Signs:

1)Battles of heaven -- Job 38:37;
2)Lions -- Job 38:39;

3)Ravens -- Job 39:41;

4)Wild goats -- Job 39:1;

5)Hinds -- Job 39:1;

6)Wild ass -- Job 39:5;

7)Unicorn 39:9;

8)Peacocks --Job 39.13;

9)Ostrich -- Job 39:13;

10)Horse -- Job 39:19;

11)Hawk -- Job 39:26;

12)Eagle -- Job 39:27.

This is so powerful: Zodiac or Circle of Gods influence. Notice that birds and animals that are mentioned by God. WHY DID GOD MENTIONED THEM? IF GOD DID NOT WANT US TO KNOW ABOUT IT. The heavens declare the Glory of the Lord , glory of the Lord in different manifestations.

1 corinthians15: 39All flesh *is* not the
same flesh: but *there is* one *kind of*
flesh of men, another flesh of beasts,
another of fishes, *and* another of
birds. 40*There are* also celestial
bodies, and bodies terrestrial: but the
glory of the celestial *is* one, and the
***glory* of the terrestrial *is* another.**
41*There is* one glory of the sun, and
another glory of the moon, and

another glory of the stars: for *one* star differeth from *another* star in glory.

I AM TALKIN ABOUT THAT THE HEAVENS DECLARE THE GLORY OF THE LORD , PARTICULARLY THE GLORY OF STARS WHICH ARE RULERS THE NIGHT.

This I will just mention: other Mystery is : Universal Ocean-Bereshit 1:2-body of water existed before anything that God done started doing of creating.
****

Revelation 21:1 that particular body of water/sea will cease to exist in some part in the future .

Amos 5:26-*But ye have borne the tabernacle of your Moloch*

and Chiun your images, the star of your god,
which ye made to yourselves

In Psalm 19 we see whole thing unraveling as far as intimate relationship between heavens and ones personal life and not in any dirty perverted way but in the way that Adam and Even was impressed upon the heavens that they were naked.

Psalm 19King James Version (KJV)

19 The heavens declare the glory of God; and the firmament sheweth his handywork.

2 Day unto day uttereth speech, and night unto night sheweth knowledge.

3 There is no speech nor language, where their voice is not heard.

4 Their line is gone out through all the earth, and their words to the end of the world. In them hath he set a tabernacle for the sun,

5 Which is as a bridegroom coming out of his chamber, and rejoiceth as a strong man to run a race.

6 His going forth is from the end of the heaven, and his circuit unto the ends of it: and there is nothing hid from the heat thereof.

Look at a short expose of the Psalm19 (vv 7,8),--

"Converting," from *to return*,
as the sun in the heavens.
"Testimony," from *to repeat*,

hence, *a witness*, spoken of the sun in Psalm 89:37.

"Sure," *faithful*, as the sun (Psa 89:37).

"Enlightening," from *to give light*, as the sun (Gen 1:15,17,18; Isa 60:19; Eze 32:7).

7 The law of the LORD is perfect, converting the soul: the testimony of the LORD is sure, making wise the simple.

8 The statutes of the LORD are right, rejoicing the heart: the commandment of the LORD is pure, enlightening the eyes.

(vv 11-13),--

"Warned," from *to make light*, hence, *to teach, admonish*.

"Keeping," from *to keep, observe*, as the heavens (Psa 130:6; Isa 21:11). Or as the heavenly bodies *observe* God's ordinances.

"Errors," from *to wander*, as the planets.

"Keep back," *to hold back, restrain*.

"Have dominion over," from *to rule*. Spoken of the sun and moon in Genesis 1:18. "The sun to rule the day," &c. (Psa 136:8,9).

11 Moreover by them is thy servant warned: and in keeping of them there is great reward.

12 Who can understand his errors? cleanse thou me from secret faults.

13 Keep back thy servant also from presumptuous sins; let them not have dominion over me: then shall I be

upright, and I shall be innocent from the great transgression.

This short expose on Psalm 19 show that Gods powerful design of heaven have everything to do with our daily life and ones way of life to be close to God.

weapon of stars (Judges 5:18 – 5:23 Judges Chapter 5

18 Zebulun and Naphtali [were] a people
[that] jeoparded their lives unto the
death **in the high places of the field.**

19 The kings came [and] fought, then
fought the kings of Canaan in Taanach
by the waters of Megiddo; they took no
gain of money.

20 They fought from heaven; the stars in
their courses fought against Sisera.

21 The river of Kishon swept them
away(terestial authority) that ancient
river, the river Kishon. O my soul, thou
hast trodden down strength.

22 Then were the horsehoofs broken by
the means of the pransings, the
pransings of their mighty ones.

23 Curse ye Meroz, said the angel of the
LORD, curse ye bitterly the inhabitants
thereof; because they came not to the
help of the LORD, to the help of the
LORD against the mighty.))

North

Dan-The
Scorpion
(Scorpio)

Asher
(Sagittarius)

Naphtali
(Capricorn)

West		**East**
Ephraim-The Bull (Taurus)	Levi (Libra)	Judah-The Lion (Leo)
Manasseh-The Bull (Taurus)	The Scales	Issachar (Cancer)
Benjamin (Gemini)		Zebulun (Virgo)

South

Reuben-The Man (Aquarius)

Simeon (Pisces)

Gad (Aries)

HEAVENS BEEN THERE FROM VERY BEGINNING FOR ALL ; This is formula is evident even in disposition of tribes, from heavens down. Key Word is " From Heavens Down!!!!!"

As it states in Romans 1 that all mankind are without excuse heavens done did declared the glory of the Lord.

Exodus 8:19
Then the magicians said to Pharaoh, "This is the finger of God." - references to creation.
All forms of witchcraft are forbidden by the high order of Apostle Oleg MB. Including astrology, horoscopes, palm readings and etc.

In Sacred **Astronomy** – **creation explanation as the stars give it to us; laws of stars. Those laws are ordained by God to praise God**
THE COMMAND WHICH ORDAINED FOR MAN TO

MANDATE UPON heavenly bodies:

Psalm 148:3 Praise you him, sun and moon: praise him, all you stars of light.

DAVID COMMANDED THE STARS AND THE MOON

Man commands the moon and the stars; David talked with stars and moon.

When you be quiet rocks will cry out. NOT ONLY HUMANS TALK TO MATTER , BUT MATTER TALKS TO!!!!!!!!!

Psalm 4:4 Stand in awe, and sin not: commune with your own heart on your bed, …

Command ye me about the works of my hands – JUST DO IT. Stars,

Reuben, 'boiling over with water,' is Aquarius (the Water Bearer)

Simeon and Levi, 'the brethren,' are Gemini (the Twins)

Judah,'the lion's whelp,' is Leo (the Lion)

Zebulon, 'who shall dwell at the beach of the sea,' is Pisces (the Fishes)

Issachar, 'a gelded donkey lying down in the cattle pens (REB)' is Taurus (the Bull)

Dan, 'a serpent in the way,' is Scorpio (the Scorpion)

Gad, 'a troop shall press upon him; but he shall press upon their heel,' is Aries (the Ram). [Aries, sun and moon fulfilling their praise by accomplishing their purpose in all they have been created to be and to do.

Infinite understanding Psalm147:5 Isaiah 34:16 Seek from the book of the LORD, and read: Not one of these will be missing; None will lack its mate. For His mouth has commanded, And His Spirit has gathered them.

EACH STAR HAS A #

EACH STAR HAS A NAME

Psalm 147:4King James Version (KJV)

4 He telleth the number of the stars; he calleth them all by their names. ABIGEL SAID name character function

AS HIS NAME SO IS HE – talking about husband Nabal=foolish

Stars have name=characteristics, they are the sign they provide the purpose for which they have been created for.

There was a star signifying the birth of Jesus. The truth is that there is a star for each of us born here on this earth.

I do not believe in astrology but in sacred astronomy. Astronomy is study of stars and constellations and their positions in heavens also now knowing the Bible scriptures that talk about the stars; one can see that role of stars and moon and the sun is instrumental part within the creation under them.

For they sun, moon and stars are there to rule the day and to rule the night. Which is time, chronology and not only that but moon influences tides, lunar calendar was prescribed by God that Jews would follow the moon. When it was new moon there was new moon celebration so forth and so on. Gregorian calendar was introduced by bloody bath.

“he will change the season times” prophet Daniel-**1582 Pope Gregory**

(as to date there is debate, but its in ball park) Gregorian calendar made people stopped doing what done God told them to do. East church never participated west church which was Catholic church Popes ordinances. That Pope -introduced this commercial calendar with no spiritual aspects or consultation of Scriptures. Thus faith and believe in God created supernatural that was above us was lost. There fore soul was famished and no scriptures about stars and moon are looked down on with disgrace and negligence.

How can soul thrive in commercial non spiritual

environments that have choked the faith, supernatural and diminished function of even created things such as stars, moon and sun.

Daniel 12:3King James Version (KJV)

3 And they that be wise shall shine as the brightness of the firmament; and they that turn many to righteousness as the stars for ever and ever.

What star are you? What stars names? What part of brightness of firmament is you? All of this is made of different vibrations according to Russian Science Journal we find:

Sound is produced by the vibrations of a body and is audible if the frequency lies between 20 and 20,000 vibrations per second. Above this range the vibration is called ultrasonic, and below, subsonic.

Light

is a form of radiant energy transmitted in electromagnetic waves, which stimulate the organs of sight.

Heat

consists of the kinetic energy of the vibrational motion of mol-ecules. The more friction, the more heat. Friction and speed are the forces

Color

is simply a different rate of vibration in another octave. The

color of an object depends upon the wavelength it reflects.

Our bodies fearfully and wonderfully made.

There are celestial bodies and there is earthly bodies. You can possess characteristics of celestial bodies here on earth. **<u>That is why there is this pull in you that you do not even understand.</u>** You can pray and fast and stand upside down on your head and guess what and no change will birth that. Heaven and stars, moon and sun are God's Bible telling you stories all day long as well as night.

SOUL KNOWLEDGE

DOES YOUR SOUL KNOWETH ????

Psalms 139:14

" **<u>I am fearfully and wonderfully made marvelous are thy works; and that my soul knoweth right well!</u>**!!!!!!!!!!!"

Does your soul knoweth right well.?

NOT YOUR MIND

NOT YOUR SPIRIT

NOT YOUR HEART

NOT ANY OF WHATEVER ITS YOURS (SEE ABOVE CHAPTER

ON IT) BUT YOUR SOUL!!!!!!!!!!!!!!!!!!!!!!!

SOUL KNOWLEDGE

there is soul food, soul music yes and there is soul knowledge and no I am not talking about carnal-soul wisdom or knowledge. **Isaiah 40:26King James Version (KJV)**

26 Lift up your eyes on high, and behold who hath created these things, **<u>that bringeth out their host by number: he calleth them all by</u>**

names by the greatness of his might, for that he is strong in power; not one faileth.

This knowledge is fail-proof.

Isaiah 42:5
Thus says God the LORD, Who created the heavens and stretched them out, Who spread out the earth and its offspring, **Who gives breath to the people on it And spirit to those who walk in it,**

We are building from stars down just as the Pyramids were built;

and not from the earth up
even as Solomon temple- even though it was the shadow of things of heavenly temple was destroyed. It was destroyed because of sin aka

disobeying Gods laws, aka building from heavens down.

This is what soul knowledge (sanctified soul) through the word of God based upon Psalms 139:14 This is not the same as in James 3- very different.

Job 9:8-10King James Version

8 Which alone spreadeth out the heavens, and treadeth upon the waves of the sea.

9 Which maketh Arcturus, Orion, and Pleiades, and the chambers of the south.

10 Which doeth great things past finding out; yea, and wonders without number.

Job 38:31King James Version (KJV)

31 Canst thou bind the sweet influences of Pleiades, or loose the bands of Orion?

Influences of Pleiades are real

and so are the bands of Orion!!!!!!!!

Binding and Loosing
Fully vested
with a belt of Orion
I have girded you with belt of Orion
omg (see in person for explaining this mystery;)
that is why we are seeking him
God, God of the stars
we are smarter than children of this world.

Amos 5:8King James Version
8 Seek him that **maketh the seven stars and Orion, and turneth the shadow of death into the morning**, and maketh the day dark with night: that calleth for the waters of the sea, and poureth them out upon the face of the earth: The LORD is his name.

A WORD OF DEATH OR SHADOW OF DEATH:

Shadow of death- absence of the stars in acts – we did not see moon stars or the sun. Acts27:20

-It took Jesus 3 days to walk through the valley of shadow of death. Death is has many different points to it. It is enemy, it is experience, it is some kind of duration and for different people it is different amount of time needed to be involved with this entity called death.

-different people have different durations and different distances because in death there is life and purpose of life in the duration called death: according to the mission that person has in his or her death and not just in this life.

Little later about this, but the fact of the matter is that no everyone even in death will be equal some dead do not know a thing, like it says in Ecclesiastes other dead people seem to do just fine and communicate and travel and etc. So it Is not that Bible contradicts itself – but it is that according to what person has achieved in this life in his personal self development.

For Example Rich and Lazarus were communicating after they have passed on to a next life. Because different people will be at different stages, in different conditions and with different abilities. So some dead know and communicate and other dead do not know anything. Endless possibilities to what universal conditions you have allowed yourself to meet and this how you will be behaving in the state or duration called Tenetas or death.

In the book of revelation there is power verse about stars and the woman, lets consider it:

Revelation 12:1King James Version (KJV)

12 And there appeared a great wonder in heaven; **a woman clothed with the sun,** and the moon under her feet, and upon her head a **crown of twelve stars:**

angelic hosts called thrones
Jacobs letter gird your lions with belt of Orion.

Heavens declare the glory of the lord and speak day to day binding and loosing strong man

Psalm 19King James Version (KJV)

19 The **heavens declare the glory
of God**; and the firmament sheweth
his handywork.

2 **Day unto day uttereth speech**,
and **night unto night sheweth
knowledge.**

**3 There is no speech nor
language, where their voice is not
heard.**

4 Their line is gone out through all
the earth, and their words to the end
of the world. **In them hath he set a
tabernacle for the sun,**

5 Which is as a **bridegroom
coming out of his chamber**, and
rejoiceth as a **strong man to run a**

race. (call out bridegroom of each month)

6 His going forth is from the end of the heaven, and his circuit unto the ends of it: and there is nothing hid from the heat thereof.

Supernatural manifestation of the thing least expected from the place least expected Job 29:6
Vs5;- strong man build the Pyramids that is why they are still standing

Chapter 5
Sacred geometry

Seven Liberal Arts:

Astronomy, Music, Geometry, Numerology, Logic, Grammar,

and Rhetoric. These sciences were thought only to Elite. ELITE ONLY!!!!!!!!!

is right knowledge going to the wrong hands and minds?

SURVILE OR SERVIAL ARTS WERE GIVEN TO TRADES PEOPLE AND THOSE WHO WHERE EMPLOYABLE.

THIS IS NOT SURVILE ARTS LADIES AND GETLEMEN!!!!!!! THESE ARE LIBERAL ARTS. LIBERAL ARTS ARE ONLY TO THOSE WHO ARE TRULY LIBERAL BECAUSE THEY HAVE BEEN LIBERATED!!!!!!!!

THE PURPOSE OF SURVILE ARTS ARE NOT TO CULTIVATE CRITICAL THINIKING BUT TO GIVE SPACIFIC SKILLS REQUIRED BY FARMERS, SMITHS, INDUSTRY OF CARPENTERS AND STONEMASONS.

Let start with basics

Sacred Geometry was all over the Cathedrals of England and other ancient so called Christians temples buildings and other architectural designs. As imperfect and manipulative nature they were done great wrong to by England and other governments.

For example:

"Dissolution of the Monasteries At the start of the Dissolution of the Monasteries in 1536, there were over 850 monasteries, nunneries and friaries in England. By 1541, there were none. More than 15,000 monks and nuns had been dispersed **and the buildings had been seized by the Crown to be sold off or**

leased to new lay occupiers.
Glastonbury Abbey was reviewed as having significant amounts of silver and gold as well as its attached lands.[56] In September 1539, the abbey was visited by Richard Layton, Richard Pollard and Thomas Moyle, who arrived there without warning on the orders of Thomas Cromwell. The abbey was stripped of its valuables[57] and Abbot Richard Whiting (Whyting), who had been a signatory to the Act of Supremacy that made Henry VIII the head of the church, resisted and was hanged, drawn and quartered as a traitor on Glastonbury Tor on 15 November 1539."

according to Wikipedia.

850 MONASTERIES

15,000 MONKS AN NUNS

AND NOT TO TAKE INTO CONSIDERATION ALL THE GOLD SILVER, LANDS AND CASH

GOD SAITH ENGLAND YOU WILL PAY FOR IT YOU AND YOUR CHILDREN CHILDREN UNTIL YOU WILL PAY UP IN FULL PLUS 20%

I am interested in the curiosity of Angels and Holy Spirit in how sacred geometry is in bedded in sacred structural designs.

YOU MEAN TO TELL ME THAT GOD DONE FORGOTTEN ABOUT IT!!!!!!!!

Abominations of so called architectures on church buildings.

Having traveled these United states and having examined these so called cultural institutions as well as religious monuments of establishments.

For example our nations capitol Washington District of Columbia has a structural design of a new Jerusalem in sacred geometry. Templar cross is all over the Washington DC. Federal triangle as it is known contains the most of Zodiacs signs than anywhere in the world. Constellation Flower of life is in the tree of life constellation is lay out of District of Columbia (that is built from the heavens down). There is fruit of flower of life. Gematria is used greatly in this city's lay out, its buildings and structures. I believe it has its truth in Bible and church History. Washington monument and pyramid are fitting in perfectly (see me in person).

This will suffice for now to arouse your interest that it is well grounded. I am not going to say that neither demonstrate the the most holy writ of revelation here fully and in all aspects.) **There are many symbols that are used in church buildings by different architecture designers which program certain destinations of humans in geometrical planes as well as releasing specific vibrations which are frequencies that are broadcasting that specific design and the agenda of architect.** And no I am not talking about crosses that would be fine and all would be well. But when it is full blown perverse rhetoric on geometrical plane it is from east to west and north to south and **people be magnetized by them. What is permissible and acceptable is like puzzle because it is only seen if you know what to look for.** In other words it is right there before your eyes and in the plane sight only it is not in words but in words of geometrical concepts and images. Images that could be interpreted in two ways (not always) and that is why it is permissible being excused as art, design and simply architecture. The subject of Sacred Geometry is extinct and non existent to point out , explain and condemn this type of subliminal, if you will, and influential *with out resistance spread of artistic geometrical witchcraft.* People in authority in the high places allow this in multi million dollar building projects referencing this type of geometrical evil as simply architecture and fine design for our warship facility.

In the late sixth century BC Pythagorean number theory linked numbers and their symbolic meanings to specific geometric shapes. THIS is I might say how it all relates to u and me. **Shapes and architectural designs is language** that few speak and thus vibration of this secret language is being broadcast ed meaning controlling atmosphere yes the very air you breath well, not really but almost really. Should I go back to Pyramids? I might., Pyramids as many other cultural and or architectural structure are and or portals, vibrational objects,

Concluding Chapter :

My remarks:

My company
1my older brother Jesus and his blood
2Holy Ghost
3Almighty God himself
4my personal angel
5the angel of my family
6the angel of my ministry
7my sister Wisdom
8my brother Discernment
9I am buddy of Bridegroom
10 strong man(+) is my friend

My Matrix in 3 Gematrias

oleg in Jewish Gematria Equals: **82** (o l e g)

50 20 5 7
o l e g

oleg in English Gematria Equals: **234** (————)

90 72 30 42
o l e g

oleg in Simple Gematria Equals: **39** (————)

15 12 5 7

Genesis 1:14

we know here that stars are there for signs . 12 signs of Zodiac.

Judges 5:17-20

17Gilead abode beyond Jordan: and **why did Dan remain in ships?** ....19**The kings came and fought, then fought the kings of Canaan in Taanach** by the waters of Megiddo; they took no gain of money. 20They fought from heaven; the stars in their courses fought against Sisera. 21The *river of Kishon swept them away, that ancient river, the river Kishon.* **O my soul, thou hast trodden down strength.** 22Then were the horsehoofs broken by the means of the pransings, the pransings of their mighty ones.

23Curse ye Meroz, said the angel of the LORD, curse ye bitterly the inhabitants thereof; because they came not to the help of the LORD, to the help of the LORD against the mighty.

It all came from God stars and moon as well as others were just celestial bodies or just a filters or managers of all Gods creation.

5) **7/13/2015- 2pm- Celestial announcement of higher hierarchy I make my self yielding vessel to spiritual righteousness, holiness, chastity in high places**: I speak to you entity that has 40,000 souls at your disposal, **loose my name, erase my name from all reachable data bases that would try to use me to harm me, entrance me and otherwise to subjecting me to perplotiv zhyttyah and all other manners of harassment .** You already lost, the blood of the Most exalted one JESUS in rank, position, stature, power, has one Yeshuah Da Ha Mashia h, He said: I all authority has been given to me in heaven all levels of it, earth = terestial realm and hell I took the key from it,,, that same

power I have given you all the power over all the power of the enemy, over all and every of all times . Today …/../.... - I accept that invitation, and also anointing. initiation into the rank of mighty ones,.,, I humbly say in response to invitation of promotion that came from the Lord

Psalm 75:6-8King James Version (KJV)

6 For promotion cometh neither from the east, nor from the west, nor from the south.

7 But God is the judge: he putteth down one, and setteth up another.

I humbly receive it!!!!! let my Angel go ahead of me and supervise it in all manners of future matters of spiritual, physical, financial, sociological, opulent, celestial terestial, mental, soulish, sexuality,.,., this is mighty wind that would not stop blowing until all my enemies will be under my feet and kings, and Queens will entreat my favor with all dimensional provisions in all capacities and in all areas they will come to me with gifts, surprises, spices, perfumes, colognes, delicacies, particular treasures of kings, and their resources, I have unlimited favor in my domain , I am irresistible!!!! ability to negotiated deals on grand scale with influences of it that would go beyond the regions of my domains. Let my restful sleep be the laboratory of growth, expedition, intervention, exploration of the unknown magnitude of man kind " fo you giveth sleep to your beloved..." Let my people go!!!!!!!!!.,. In this anointing initiation let the enemies will recognize and submit to me with out resistance to my position, rank, allotted authority that has been invested in me this day ../../,,., at 2pm.,. No one will oppose me in their consciousness, let good will towards me prevail in every heart, soul, mind body, spirit,.,, etc.,,.. . I effortlessly rule over them, in all arenas of life effortlessly enforcing my rule using all weaponry of the house,.,

I got hold of God in all dimensions at all times under full protection, I here by submit to order , structures, righteous dominions powers rulers I realize my rank and thankful for this opportunity of promotion on that grand scale of Gods omnipotent exuberant and extravagant grace which knows no boundaries of time, space, and all other measurements known or unknown, I belong to you Yeshuah Ha Mashia h ,., and to the order of your holy ones in all manner, aspects, and structures and other orderly provision of your kingdom., according to the order of Melchizadek. All parts of this temple is subdued to your governing authority at all times in all areas by all to whom I come into contact with. From this day forward your name will be Al Oleg Bar Jonah (look up the # who do not know the left from right 120,000;;; 3x40,000) and your manifestation of MY glory at this level will be unparalleled to anything you have seen heard or experienced. Behold I am creating a new thing, totally new,.,,, no words to it no theology to it,., no ecclesiastical order to it.,., my Davidic warship became religion..,. Wild man of God who has not been domesticated by all spiritual wickedness in high places. Al Oleg Bar Jonah / Dove. In order for you to be in recognized in this level of perpetual

authoritative alignment you have to have new name of domain. Domain of
40,000 40,0000 40,000

Domain of 120,000 of my grace, mercy, providence, provision, unrecognized yet mystery of the treasuries of my Hockmah. You are Al Oleg Bar Dove are invested in this domain and spiritual righteousness in high places. With effortless manifestation of all that pertains to your office, space, wealth, opulence at all times in all celestial dealings and terrestrial life and encounters. You are enabled with all provisions of yourself and all extensions of yourself, things, people, angels, yet to be discovered entities at all times in all realms of your domain. I am just but a lad oh governing angel and MY Lord Jesus Christ., this pack makes me in your presence to tremble and fall on the knees of my heart and be speechless.,,, you are now beginning the live the portion of your life of heaven here on earth.,.,. You will have people, places and every realm in your domain under control of your rule OZRYUWZIR. When you will say a word, it will happen and it will manifest instantly shortly and rapidly and with out resistance and opposition of parties that are contrary in their ignorance that they have despised the authorities.

WE ARE NOT TO BURN INCENSE OR WORSHIP ANY OF GODS CREATION AS WE SEE IN THIS NEXT SCRIPTURES........2 Kings 23:5King James Version (KJV)

5 And he put down the idolatrous priests, whom the kings of Judah had ordained to burn incense in the

high places in the cities of Judah, and in the places round about Jerusalem; them also that burned incense unto Baal, to the sun, and to the moon, and to the planets, and to all the host of heaven.

King James Version

2 Peter 2:10

But chiefly them that walk after the flesh in the lust of uncleanness, and despise government. Presumptuous are they, self willed, they are not afraid to speak evil of dignities.

God works in generational order, dynasty is not theory is Who God is and this is what he wants for us!!!!!!!!!!!!!!!!!!!!!

who is shem ? And why would you care it?

shem was only one individual who knew the life before and after the flood.

Shem was one individual whose life overlapped with Abraham (When you meet any person; ask God in you how deep is that person? What is the genealogy of their spirituality, wealth, health, soul depth? Some person is deep 1000 generations. I take every day that my ancestors did not get to live, I take everyday that they have wasted (and live it), you can live the lives that they did not take possession to live: see me in person to go further in it, **I can access into peoples DNA and consciousness and rewrite their hard drive or their destiny (Jacob did it, Moses did it, Deborah did it) .** that is what Absalom was doing it says steal the hearts of man - peoples

So my summary of this book **Genesis:...**"Who *told* thee that thou wast naked?" Psalm 97:6, "The heavens *declare* His righteousness"; The heavens started to talk to Adam and Even and told them that they were naked as the result from sin as opposed to naked covered by the glory of God 111:6, "*He hath shewed* his people the power of his works." The heavens done did declare to the Adam and Eve that they were naked as result of their violation of what was forbidden by God.

www.ingramcontent.com/pod-product-compliance
Ingram Content Group UK Ltd.
Pitfield, Milton Keynes, MK11 3LW, UK
UKHW041934190726
13854UKWH00004B/1584

9 781387 395927